"
Unschooling: Birth Through Early Elementary" is a book in the Modern Alternative Mama collection. Other books in this collection:

- Real Food Basics
- Healthy Pregnancy Super Foods
- Against the Grain: Delicious Recipes for Whole Food and Grain-Free Diet
- Treat Yourself: Real Food Desserts
- Wholesome Comfort: Whole Foods to Warm and Nourish Your Family
- Breast to Bib: Modern Alternative Mama's Guide to Nourishing Your Growing Baby
- Simply Summer
- A Practical Guide to Children's Health
- Healing with God's Earthly Gifts: Natural and Herbal Remedies

Copyright ©2015 | Kate Tietje, Modern Alternative Mama, LLC

Cover Design and layout by Casey Spitnale, www.hellovoom.com.

...Table of Contents...

Introduction

Unschooling is becoming a more popular method of homeschooling as a lot of parents step away from traditional forms of "school" and look for what really works for their families. This is especially popular in the early years, when kids learn best through play and exploration.

A lot of families understand the general idea behind unschooling -- although some have some misconceptions -- but many aren't sure where to actually start. They need a practical guide to what unschooling looks like, and ideas to start with. That's what this guide is for.

Before you jump to the actual activities and ideas, be sure

to read through this introductory section to get a feel for what unschooling is and why it's done. Especially in the preschool years, it may seem like the unschooling ideas offered are "what all good parents do." And, to some extent, that's true! Not a lot is required in the early years for kids to learn.

It's about the ideas, the deliberate interaction, the general philosophy. If you're new to unschooling, jump in to learn more!

What is Unschooling?

• •

"Unschooling" is a philosophy about learning through living, rather than using a formal curriculum. The goal is that a lot of important skills and knowledge can be learned through daily life, and that sit-down "school" is not necessary. Many even believe that modern schooling methods are against a child's natural development and can be detrimental.

The most important tenet of unschooling is that it is child-led. The child shows an interest in a particular subject or area, and the parents help the child to fully explore that interest. This is in sharp contrast to more traditional methods of schooling, where a parent or teacher chooses the curriculum and "assignments" and the children complete them.

Unschooling allows a child to work on an area of interest when they are developmentally ready to do so, rather than when some external source says they should. Some children will learn to read at 3 or 4; others do not learn to read until 8 or 9 (and once they do learn, they do quite well and have no "developmental delay").

It also allows for children to learn in a way that makes the most sense to them. Some children enjoy doing written work; others need to be hands-on; some need to sing; and so on. Each child thinks a bit differently and unschooling allows them to learn how they think and tailor their educational approach to it. Some children might end up thinking they are dumb if they have to fit into a particular mold; when in fact the issue is that they simply approach a topic differently.

There is a range of "unschooling" that goes on; not all families approach it the same way. Since it's child-led, this isn't surprising. What some might consider too rigid is the perfect approach for others. There is generally sort of a spectrum that goes on, from 'radical' unschooling to a more mixed approach.

Ultimately, if you choose a child-led approach and a relaxed attitude towards formal curriculum, you may be an "unschooler." It depends on what your family chooses!

What is Radical Unschooling? (Is All Unschooling Radical?)

As I mentioned in the previous section, there's a continuum of unschooling, from "radical" to a more mixed/balanced approach.

"Radical unschooling" is usually defined as absolutely no curriculum or attempts at formal teaching. No lessons, no classes, nothing that most would consider "school." The idea is that any and all learning that is needed will occur through the normal activities of life.

Most unschoolers, including our family, are more "moderate" unschoolers. That is, no formal curriculum is chosen (especially in the early years) and there is little external guidance -- it's mostly child-led learning. But, when children express an interest in a particular subject or area, parents specifically seek to help them learn all they can about it. This includes books, possibly textbooks, movies, field trips, and more. Nothing is "off limits" even if it is more typical of "formal schooling" so long as the child has an interest in it.

What that means is, these families do have workbooks. They do have flashcards. They do have lots of educational books, field trips, and chances to work one-on-one with their children. It's just that they do these things because the child sought it out, not because the parent decided it was "time" or that it was the best way.

This sort of unschooling walks the line between "radical unschooling" and more formal homeschooling. This is the general philosophy upon which this book is based -- a moderate approach.

The bottom line is that you don't have to be "radical" to be considered an unschooler.

Why Unschool?

You still may be wondering -- "But why would anyone un-school? Sure, in the early years, learning should be play-based; we all know that. But later, they must have formal study to learn."

I ask you -- why do you think so?

Formal learning starting around age 5 or 6 is what we're used to. But that doesn't mean it's the only way. Or the best way.

Consider -- is there value in making a child do busy work? Is there long-term value in "making" a child learn

from a particular book if they don't want to? Will they actually gain knowledge, and if so, will they retain it?

Studies show they don't.

When people are forced to "learn" things they aren't very interested in, they may remember it long enough to take a test and regurgitate the information. But they will later forget most of it. They will not incorporate it into how they think, and they will not change how they learn because of it.

In other words, no real "learning" has taken place. Memorizing information temporarily isn't learning.

The goal of unschooling is real learning. That is, for a child to truly understand a subject or area and to grow as a person and expand their understanding of the world around them. The goal is for them to assimilate the new information into their future learning, without the threat (promise?) of tests or grades.

This sort of authentic learning is much easier to get with unschooling, or any sort of education that can be tailored to a child's needs and learning styles, than in a setting where this is not possible. If learning is expected to progress by "grade levels," where the child is supposed to meet (and not too far exceed) certain benchmarks in several subjects, and this is to be measured by standardized testing, then we don't really know what a child truly understands. This a poor substitute for authentic learning.

Unschooling isn't the only way to achieve authentic learning, but it's one way that does work -- very well, for some families.

We know that if any aspect of unschooling weren't working for some members of our family at any point, we would change it up until we found something that did work. Unschooling isn't a rigid philosophy, and it does require quite a lot of involvement from the parents, to be done well. It requires continuous play, quiet assessment, and constant exposure to new experiences.

But it's worth it, to see the joy that children feel in learning because they want to, and not because they're being pressured to "have" to learn. It's awesome to see their natural curiosity take over. For them to not even understand the concept of "being tired of school." To know that regardless of their strengths and weaknesses, their needs can be met. That's why unschooling is great!

When Does Unschooling Start?

Unschooling, as a philosophy, can start as early as birth -- and this book is geared towards those early years.

The idea is that learning never "starts" and it never "stops." A baby is learning from the moment they are born about the world around them.

A newborn learns that when their tummy feels funny, they cry, they are fed, and that feeding helps them feel better. Thus, they learn that being held + food solves the funny feeling, which they learn is hunger.

A baby learns when they cry, someone comes to pick them up and soothe them. They learn to trust that someone will come and help them when they cry.

An older baby learns to grab objects. Then, to drop them -- and see who will pick them up! They find their hands and feet and examine them. They learn to look at different types of patterns and colors and make sense of them. Even young infants are more drawn to face-like patterns than other types.

Since "unschooling" is a philosophy that espouses learning through daily life, all of these normal daily activities are unschooling!

Of course, as children get more into the preschool and early elementary years, there's more to learn beyond just living life (although that's still important, too).

Unschooling never really starts or ends, though, and that's why this book covers the early years, starting from birth and ending around age 7 - 8.

If you don't personally feel that anything is required in the earliest years, or don't want to think about "education" yet, that's okay! Start whenever you feel comfortable. It's never too late. But, read this book with an open mind. A lot of the activities that we're suggesting work well for families who don't want to start too soon. They're very flexible and open-ended.

Our Unschooling Story

We always knew that we would homeschool our children.

I had done "okay" in public school (quite well in my later years, actually) and my husband, Ben, had been homeschooled. His family was more of the "I need a plan" type, so they did follow a formal curriculum, but he had a lot of flexibility within it. As long as he completed his assignments each week, and tests as needed, he could budget his time however he wanted and do whatever he pleased with the time leftover. He spent quite a bit of time reading books, watching educational TV, and taking apart and reassembling the family computer!

When our oldest was an infant, we first ran across the idea of "unschooling." It strongly appealed to us, because both of us are very much self-starters, leaders, and we like to think outside the box and do things our way. Striking out on our own instead of following a purchased curriculum seemed like it would fit really well for our family.

Our oldest is now 7, and we have three others (5.5, 3.5, 2) and we're expecting our fifth this summer! We've had quite a bit of experience with unschooling now that our oldest two are nearly through the "first grade" and "kindergarten" years. (Not that they have any idea about "grades." They honestly do not know how to answer the question "What grade are you in?")

In the early years, we did very little with them that was for-

mal. We read to them. We talked about shapes and colors.
We had them work alongside us in the kitchen, doing the
laundry, and so on.

By age 3 - 4, we started using little games, flash cards, art
supplies, and occasionally workbooks. We joined our local
zoo and a children's science museum and went fairly often.
We continued to read with them.

Our daughter's kindergarten year was devoted largely to
science and math. She showed no interest in reading and
flat-out refused to read with us most of the time, or have
anything to do with it. The first part of the year, we did
simple science experiments, visited the local museums,
watched a lot of videos on how things were made, a lot of
Magic School Bus, and so on.

In the second half of her kindergarten year, she showed a
strong interest in math. During a six-month time period,
she went from barely able to count to 20, to being able to
count into the hundreds, do 2 and 3-digit addition, basic
subtraction, telling time, counting money, and more. When
she was ready, she learned nearly two years' worth of math
curriculum in only a few months' time.

At the beginning of her first grade year, our daughter suddenly picked up an interest in reading. She had already
known all her letters and letter sounds (and had been interested in writing for a couple of years already; she would
write the handful of words she knew to make projects for
others), but she began to do sight words on flashcards daily. She would read early reader books that we bought for
her as well. In a couple of months, she was reading basic

books with our help, and picking up new words all the time. When she was ready for each subject, she tackled it with singular focus.

Our younger boys have been similar in tackling things when they're ready, but quite different in what they chose and when. Our 5.5 YO boy showed an early aptitude for design, building incredible spaceships and other items out of small Legos from age 3. (Things I'm sure I couldn't make!) He thought in pictures.

We encouraged him to do this sort of design, providing him with buckets full of Legos, which he plays with for hours each day, designing different objects. Over time his designs have progressed, so that they're now layered to be more sturdy and to incorporate moving parts.

We weren't focusing on more academic pursuits with him very much, and then one day when he was not quite 5, he sat down and wrote all of his letters, free-hand. We had no idea where he'd learned to do it. He picked up on letter sounds from little videos that sing them, and has been working in workbooks that have "missing letters" he has to fill in after sounding out the words. For him, singing and sounds has been very helpful -- sight words don't make much sense to him. This, along with early reader books on Star Wars (something else he loves) are helping him learn to read!

Our 3.5 YO son is learning constantly from his siblings. He's learned shapes and colors mostly from playing with them, or building with the wooden blocks that we have. He has an extensive vocabulary for his age and enjoys building alongside his older brother. Most of his learning is still truly play-based, although he sometimes likes to "read with us" like the older ones do!

The 2 YO enjoys getting in on some of the activity, too! He loves to name body parts and play silly games with music. He picks up our phones and TV buttons and learns to work them through observation. He likes to see what will happen if he _____ (throws something, spills something, etc.). He's a little scientist so far!

With each of them, we see their personalities and talents emerging. We play lots of games and do lots of learning activities that are appropriate for their age levels. We don't push them academically. If we had said our daughter had to learn to read during her kindergarten year, she would have been frustrated, we would have been frustrated, and we wouldn't have made much progress. But when she was ready, early in her first grade year, she leapt ahead quickly and was excited and proud -- and so were we!

A casual approach in the early years may feel like not much progress is being made. And maybe, academically, that's true. But just wait -- many kids, just like ours, will suddenly learn in leaps and bounds when they are ready. We've loved our unschooling journey so far, and have been amazed at all that we have all learned!

Section 1:
Unschooling Birth to Age 2

In this section, we're covering what unschooling looks like from birth to age 2. We'll be talking about the type of things kids this age are typically learning, what is developmentally appropriate, plus the types of activities that are good for teaching. Make sure you've read the introduction first, so that you have a good handle on the unschooling philosophy.

This age is tricky, in a way, because a newborn is vastly different from a two-year-old! But these early years are so critical for brain building, and that brain is built through exploring the world. That's what we'll be focusing on.

What Unschooling Looks Like Now

. . . .

Unschooling in this age group changes dramatically over time. A newborn needs very little specific stimulation/interaction beyond what parents typically do -- holding, snuggling, talking, smiling, and meeting their physical needs.

In the very earliest weeks, it is beneficial to hold the baby in your arms and look down at him or her. A distance of 8 - 9" from your face is ideal. Allow the baby to study your face a lot. After a few weeks, you're likely to see a smile!

Floor time is beneficial from birth, too. Your baby can lie on her back or stomach, although don't force her to stay that way if she cries. Having something interesting to look at sitting next to her or in front of/over top of her is good, too. Bold patterns and brightly contrasting colors are the best -- first in black and white, and then in dark, strong colors (pastels aren't the best for babies).

By two months of age, babies will start to bat at objects with their hands. A place to sit with objects 6 - 8" away from them is nice, so that they can stare at them and try to hit them.

By four months, babies will start to grab objects. Some will be able to sit with support. A small number may be able to sit alone. Over the next few months, they'll learn to grab objects more and more easily, laugh when others do silly things, and play games like peek-a-boo. They will also learn to sit alone, and scoot or crawl.

Once a baby is crawling (6 - 10 months), they will be putting every object in their mouths. Make sure there are plenty of safe objects -- soft, no sharp edges, no small pieces. Keep unsafe objects, especially older siblings' toys, away from them.

By a year, most babies can understand most of what you say and some are beginning to say words of their owns. They will learn to point and gesture if you demonstrate this for them. Many also have definite ideas of their own and the ability to think ahead -- a little bit. They can follow one and sometimes two-step directions. Many are very eager to "help" and "do it myself" soon after this.

By age two, babies aren't really babies anymore! They will learn to walk, run, throw, name body parts, may learn colors, and can follow two and three-step directions. They're capable of inferring "if this, then this" (i.e. if you say "We're going to the store" they might grab their shoes and rush for the door). Toddlers are learning about the world very rapidly, and in a very hands-on way.

At this age, basically, it's about allowing them the time and space they need to explore, and making sure that space is safe. An open room where cords are tucked away and there's nothing they can topple, and no small objects they could swallow is ideal -- letting them crawl and explore freely, as soon as they can. Before they're mobile, bringing them a variety of objects to explore is an excellent idea.

In the following sections, see more specific ideas!

Developmental Goals

The overarching developmental goal in this age group is "competence." That is, that infants and young toddlers develop a sense of how the world works, their place  in it, and how they can affect the world around them in an autonomous way.

Age 0 - 2 Months

At this age, baby is:

- Learning to sort out what it means to be alive
- Studying faces and face-like drawings or depictions
- Learning their family members from other people
- Learning the "social smile"
- Studying objects and patterns
- Beginning to bat at objects

Age 2 - 4 Months

At this age, baby is:

- Smiling regularly at others, encouraging social play
- Learning to laugh
- Showing preference for favorite people (usually family members)
- Trying to grab objects (but can't hold on to them long)
- Learning to sit with support

Age 4 - 6 Months

At this age, baby is:

- Grasping objects more easily
- Examining/exploring objects
- Reaching for people
- Learning to sit without support
- Showing an interest in the activities others are doing
- Learning to scoot/crawl

Age 6 - 8 Months

At this age, baby is:

- Crawling or learning to do so
- Pulling to stand
- Learning object permanence
- Learning cause and effect (i.e. "if I drop this, you'll pick it up")
- Developing separation anxiety
- Beginning to eat some solid food

Age 8 - 10 Months

At this age, baby is:

- Pulling to stand frequently
- Putting everything in their mouth
- Beginning to "cruise" on furniture
- Saying first words
- May be able to learn baby sign, if taught
- Gesturing and grunting to make wants known
- Holding up arms to be picked up
- Learns to use a cup

Age 10 - 12 Months

At this age, baby is:

Pulling to stand

- Cruising around furniture
- Taking first steps
- May be learning to use "baby sign"
- Waving, pointing, and using other gestures
- Beginning to understand most of what parents are saying
- Crawling up and down stairs
- Beginning stranger anxiety

Age 12 - 15 Months

At this age, baby is:

- Learning to walk independently and full-time
- Carrying objects while walking

- Beginning to say more words
- Able to follow 1 and 2-step directions (i.e. "Pick up that paper and throw it away")
- Understands almost all words adults say (simple/common ones)
- Eating mostly solid foods; may still be breastfeeding
- Learns to feed self with fork and spoon
- Enjoys putting small objects into holes (ex. plastic lids into a tissue box)
- Often strong stranger anxiety

Age 15 - 18 Months

At this age, baby is:

- Saying several words (usually)
- Beginning to string words into short sentences
- Follows multi-step directions
- Enjoys "helping" parents with tasks around the house
- Refines feeding skills
- Learns to run
- May learn to walk up/down stairs
- Learns to kick balls, and throw balls underhand
- Shows interest in other babies/children; engages in parallel play
- May wean (or may not!)
- Most sleep through the night

Age 18 - 24 Months

At this age, baby is:

- Speaking in short sentences more often
- Learning dozens of new words
- Practicing fine motor skills -- putting "stuff in other stuff"
- Helping around the house
- May learn to put on clothes, with some help
- May learn to remove clothes, with some help
- Learns to throw balls overhand
- Learns to scribble on paper with crayons
- Looks at books; enjoys being read to
- May watch TV, if offered
- Has much more definite likes and dislikes and expresses them

Unschooling Activities

With very young babies, there are no real activities. Spend lots of time skin-to-skin and lots of time looking into baby's face. Placing baby in your arms allows them to see you most clearly. By the time baby is 2 - 3 months old, placing baby on your legs (while you're sitting with your legs up) is fun -- baby can get a new view on the world and will likely smile at you!

Once baby can smile and interact with the world a little bit, try some of these ideas.

Tummy Time

Laying baby on his or her tummy can be a good exercise -- baby gets a new vantage point and strengthens muscles. Some babies truly hate this and scream. If your baby is one of them, don't push it -- the same muscles can be strengthened through babywearing. If your baby does enjoy it, though, even for a short time, go for it. Place interesting objects, like brightly-colored toys or mirrors (unbreakable, baby-safe ones) near baby.

Baby Massage

Lay the baby on a towel, naked (or wearing just a diaper) in a warm room so s/he won't get cold. Use a food-grade oil, like olive or coconut, to help your hands move smoothly. Use very light pressure; unlike with an adult, you're not trying to work the muscles, just stimulate the nerves. Gently run your hands down baby's arms, starting at the shoulder and moving to the fingertips. Then, do the same thing with the legs -- start at the top, move to the toes. Run your hands down baby's belly, and back (if s/he'll lay belly-down). Do a clockwise motion on baby's belly. This often relaxes babies, and being touched is very important to them at this age. Follow up with a bath with both of you in the tub together.

Hanging Toy Bar

Many babies by 2 - 3 months of age enjoy looking at hanging toys. These can be clipped onto bouncers, or set on the floor with baby lying underneath. Place them close enough that baby can bat at the toys and try to grab them. Most babies this age enjoy this activity and like the practice. Change out the toys now and then to keep their interest.

Rattles/Teethers

Once baby can hold onto objects, even for a short time (3 - 4 months), offer wooden teethers or rattles. Babies will shake them and be startled, but they will eventually connect what they do to the sound that occurs, learning cause and effect. Plus, these are objects that are safe to mouth. Many babies also like silicone-type teethers, something that is roughly the texture of human skin. (Great to offer if they are biting you!)

Empty Bowls, Cups, Spoons

Once babies can sit with support (4 - 6 months), place them in a high chair or other chair and put some toys in front of them -- empty bowls, cups, and large spoons are good. Babies will bang them together, bang them on the tray, put the spoons into the bowls, and so on. Older babies will throw them off the tray and wait for you to retrieve them! It's another cause-and-effect game. Many babies will get bored with the same objects after a little while, so swap out for new ones. Wooden spoons, measuring cups (metal or plastic), or most any non-sharp, non-breakable household item works great.

Peek-a-Boo

Around 6 - 8 months, baby begins to learn object permanence -- that things exist even when they can't see them. Use a towel or your hands to hide your face, then pop out and say "peek a boo!" This is a great game for when they haven't quite learned the concept. Many babies are surprised when you pop out and will laugh. You can do variations on this game, like hiding behind the corner and jumping out while baby is sitting somewhere safe.

Hide-The-Toy

Once a baby has learned object permanence, this is a good game. Place a toy on a tray or table that baby can reach. Cover the toy with a towel. If baby understands object permanence, she should begin to move the towel to find the toy! (If not, she'll ignore it -- it's "gone" now.)

Activity Mat

Some babies really like to play with activity mats. These usually have mirrors, wooden rings to grab, interesting patterns to look at, and so on. Place baby to lay or sit on this and see what he does with it all! Add some other toys once he can sit up and grab.

Floor Time

Lots of babies enjoy time on the floor once they can sit or crawl. Allow your baby plenty of time to be down without restrictions (except, of course, to keep cords or other not-safe things out of the way; make this a safe space for baby to explore). Baby will learn to sit, scoot, crawl, and pull to stand by practicing at his own pace. Some are easily frustrated and want to be picked up quickly; others will spend hours on the floor peacefully! Go with what your baby needs and wants. But offer floor time when you can. Leave some interesting, baby-safe objects around to grab. You can leave magazines out if you don't mind them getting ripped up. Babies often like to do that!

Climbing Time

Once your baby is crawling (8 - 10 months), try making a little obstacle course. Use small pillows and blankets to give your baby items to crawl on or around. These will be soft so that if baby falls, he won't get hurt. Some moms like to offer special "tubes" to crawl through, or actual plastic "jungle gyms" to climb on, but these aren't necessary. Boxes to climb into or put stuff in are a great idea too -- babies and children love empty boxes.

Activity Box

This one can be super simple, or complicated. There are expensive, intricate wooden boxes you can buy that allow baby to push and pull, and otherwise manipulate items. Or, you can take an empty oatmeal container and cut a small slot in the top, about ½" by 2". Give the baby large pop-sicle sticks or old plastic caps, and let the baby push them through the slot. This entertains babies for a long time! Try giving baby different sized or shaped objects to push through. Remove the lid and see how many larger objects fit inside. There are endless variations to this.

Water Play

Many babies love to play with water. Once babies can sit up well, put them in the bath tub with a few inches of water and some cups, a whisk, or other safe objects. There are baby-safe bubble baths you can use, too.

Sensory Boxes

Sensory boxes are just a name for boxes filled with items that have different textures. A box filled with rice, or beans, or even pumpkin guts could be a "sensory box." Some peo-ple choose small balls (not small enough to choke!), or even a mix of different items. Offer cups, spoons, etc. to use to play with these items too. Make sure to watch baby so that s/he doesn't swallow items that could cause choking.

Silly Songs

Babies and toddlers love silly songs. Try nursery rhymes, of games like "Head, Shoulders Knees and Toes" to get them moving. There are a number of other kids' songs that let toddlers play games with hands and bodies, too. "Eensy Weensy Spider," for example. Check on Youtube for plenty of examples.

Finger Paint

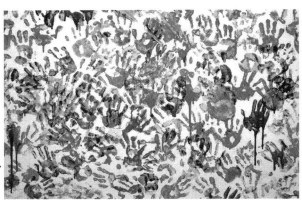

Choose a non-toxic paint for this, because it might go in the mouth! You can even choose ketchup, mustard, chocolate sauce, and other edibles as "paint" so that eating it doesn't matter. Give your baby a piece of paper (or even just a clean table) and let them smear to their heart's content. Be prepared for it to get in hair, on clothes, etc. -- it'll probably be bath time after! This would be a great outdoor activity if the weather cooperated, possibly followed by some time in a swimming pool.

Play Dough

Older toddlers will enjoy playing with play dough. There are plenty of versions you can make at home that are edible (although unpalatable). Or, you can give your child cookie dough (minus the eggs) as play dough. Offer a small rolling pin, a spoon, a fork, even a non-sharp "knife" (like a frosting spreader). Let them squish, smash, roll, and

mold. Try some different textures of "dough" to play with --
squishy, slimy, sticky, etc. so your child can experiment with
different materials.

Ball Toss

By the time baby can sit well -- around 9 - 10 months -- he'll
be able to push a ball back and forth with you. Sit on the
floor and practice rolling the ball and catching it between
your legs. Older toddlers may enjoy gentle tosses and at-
tempting to catch the ball with their hands. Big, light foam
balls are great for this, as they won't break anything or hurt
anyone. You can offer a basket or other target for your little
one to throw the ball into, as well.

Paper Ripping

Babies love to play with paper. Give your child a pile of
scrap paper and allow them to crumble or rip it up. Older
toddlers may enjoy sticking the ripped paper to a sheet of
contact paper or a piece of paper you have spread with a
glue stick to create "art." Make sure to watch little ones
around glue or glue sticks -- many will try to eat it.

Unschooling Materials

· ·

There are a bunch of different materials you can use for young babies and toddlers. We'll break it down a little bit by age.

Ages 0 - 12 Months

- Wooden teethers
- Rattles
- Cups
- Bowls
- Spoons
- Non-sharp kitchen tools
- Empty bottles
- Empty boxes

Ages 12 - 24 Months

- Boxes
- Paper
- Magazines (for ripping/looking)
- Soft foam balls
- Edible or non-toxic paints
- Large crayons
- Play dough
- Water
- Baskets
- Washable markers

What Our Family Does At This Age

• •

Since we have so many kids, our littles are fully integrated into our family life from day 1! Brand new babies are carried in arms or carriers as we go through our daily routines -- meals, play time, bedtime. We started this with our third child.

Small babies are held or rocked by multiple family members (parents, siblings, grandparents), as well as talked to and played with. By two months, babies are sitting in bouncers while siblings talk and tickle. Often first laughs are because of sibling silliness!

Older babies sit up in high chairs to join us for meals and other activities. They are offered non-sharp kitchen tools to play with while the older kids are involved in a baking project or cleaning up -- where they can see us and be a part of what is going on (this is around 4 - 5 months to start).

Mobile babies are encouraged to crawl around after siblings, and play peek-a-boo games with them. Our third child, around 9 months, hid behind the legs of our kitchen table while he almost 3-year-old brother peeked around while they both laughed.

Young toddlers are given jobs -- fetching small, non-breakable items, putting away towels, putting spoons into or taking out of the dishwasher, and so on. They are usually very eager to help! It's safer to give them a job than to see what they try to take on. My little ones would go straight for the knives or other unsafe things if I didn't give them a safe job fast enough!

We spend a lot of time listening to the little ones. By 18 months or so, they have very definite opinions about what they do and don't like. We can diffuse most tantrums by getting down on their level and asking them what it is they want. They don't always get it, but we can ask and then say "No, that's not safe, let's do this instead" or "Yes, I can do that for you." Very often this stops the tantrums before they start, because they know we understand.

Tantrums are far more likely when we don't know what they want and try to dismiss them because we are busy. Many requests are very simple anyway and are no problem to fulfill -- one of my toddlers was really particular about wanting ice in his water!

We do a lot of outdoor play once they can crawl, and we encourage them to play on playgrounds, climb up short ladders and go down slides. We encourage stair climbing, too, as long as we are behind them in case they fall. We visit indoor play areas that are padded and let them go nuts!

Basically, we encourage them to explore the world in a safe manner, with lots of parental and sibling interaction.

Section 2:
Unschooling Age 2 - 4

Toddlers at this age take a pretty big developmental leap, too, although not as big as in the first two years! Two year olds are still learning to talk and learning to become independent, and they tend to be pretty clumsy still. Four year olds talk smoothly and readily and are very independent in many ways. Each age has its own benefits -- and drawbacks!

Your child is growing mentally much faster than he is growing physically now, which is important. A newborn will quadruple or more in size by age 2 and makes major leaps in their gross motor skills. But between ages 2 and 4, children won't grow nearly as much, and they won't make as much progress in their gross motor skills. Instead, their cognitive and fine motor skills take over!

This means it's time for "real learning." (Everything is really "real learning" but this is more of the academic-type learning that we think of when we say "learning.") A lot of parents get excited and want their kids to start learning all of their shapes, colors, numbers, and letters. Most children will learn these things during this age range...but they don't need you to push them, to do it. They will learn very naturally.

Toddlers and preschoolers also become very capable. They can feed themselves fairly neatly. They learn to use the toilet. They learn to dress themselves. They learn to be more helpful than hindering around the house, in small ways. They can fool you....

Preschoolers are still very emotional and immature at times -- even by age 4. They can still become easily overwhelmed by the world and melt down. They still need a lot of love and guidance from you. It may surprise you at times, how quickly they can go from confident and independent to curled up on your lap, bawling. It's a feature of the age!

Remember this as you walk through this portion of your unschooling journey. They'll learn best with an environment that's open to them, that is moving at their pace, that allows them to explore the world in a way that makes sense to them. They don't react well to being asked to sit still or be quiet, or being led to learn the way someone else wants. They can get overwhelmed by too many activities or being pushed too hard. Leave their world open -- they'll learn more, and they'll be happy to do it.

What Unschooling Looks Like Now

Unschooling in the toddler and preschool years becomes much more academic -- but not too academic. It's about learning about the world around them, and what they're capable of.

Kids will start to ask "What is that?" and then "Why?" quite a lot, as they learn to talk better. They will want to know about everything around

them! "Why do dogs have four legs?" "Where do rainbows come from?" "Why are garden slugs slimy?"

One of the very best things you can do is to answer them!

You may not know the answers to all their questions. Say, "Let's find out together." Use books, videos, and other resources to learn about the world, and to answer the questions that they have. They will pick up on so much this way -- and you can be assured that if they're asking, they want to know!

This is a good time to provide your child with a lot of experiences that will help them learn. Trips to the playground to practice their motor and social skills are a good idea.

Trips to the library will help them learn and you can take books home to learn even more. Trips to children's museums where they can touch, look, and explore are excellent too! (Trips to more traditional adults' museums where it's a look-but-don't-touch deal will likely be met with boredom at this age.)

Take advantage of local resources. Visit parks. Have play dates with like-minded friends. Be sure to enjoy the world!

At home, it's good to have a selection of quality toys, now that they have opinions about which ones they truly like and enjoy. Follow your child's interests. Some love Legos or Duplos; some love wooden trains; some love toy kitchens; some are really into art supplies. I'm a fan of limiting toys to 2 - 3 favorite choices rather than having "toy soup" everywhere.

You can also choose to swap out toys for new ones every couple of weeks -- have a closet or other place where you keep different sets of toys in boxes and rotate. We do some of this and have heavy-duty plastic totes with lids to keep the sets not in use.

In a Perfect World, I would have a home with three or four different "play rooms," each with their own theme. There would be a House Playroom, with a realistic toy kitchen with utensils, a small table and chairs, dolls and accessories, dress up clothes, and other related items. In another area would be several different sets of building blocks -- Legos, wooden blocks, you name it. In another would be massive art supplies -- paper in all colors, crayons, paint, tape, glue, recycled items, and more. All of these items would stay beautifully in their "homes" except what was being played with, quietly and nicely, and it would all be cleaned up before moving on to the next activity.

Real life doesn't work like that, so we limit toys. It actually increases their creativity to have less! My kids often grab empty boxes to "make something new." Choose whichever way works for your home, but remember -- sometimes less is more!

Developmental Goals

Your child is changing quite a lot, cognitively, at this stage. We'll break it down by years.

Ages 2 - 3 Years

- Learns to use the toilet
- Learns to recognize letters (often times)
- Learns to count to 5 or 10
- Identifies colors
- Identifies body parts
- Begins to speak in longer, more complex sentences
- By age 3, most speech is understandable
- Learns to kick balls
- Learns to climb easily
- Begins to ask questions frequently
- Can feed self with little mess
- Becomes more helpful
- Explores the world like a "little scientist," testing things

Ages 3 - 4 Years

- Speech becomes even more complex and vocabulary increases
- Asks questions very frequently -- some say more than 400 a day!
- Begins to develop friendships/cooperative play instead of parallel play
- May show an interest in learning to read (many do not; average age is 3 - 9 years)
- Begins to do rudimentary math (i.e. counting in the grocery store, adding small numbers)
- May stop napping
- Remembers things long-term
- Can tell stories about recent and long-term memories ("remember that time...")
- Classifies objects and makes assumptions based on prior knowledge

Unschooling Activities

• •

At this age, there are a ton of activities kids can do! Make sure to adjust these for your child's particular age and needs. Some are more cautious than others, and they all have different interests. Let your creative juices flow, and follow your child's lead! These are ideas to get you started but by no means is this an exhaustive list!

Cooking and Baking Projects

Many kids love to help in the kitchen. They can join you in the kitchen at this age, and can learn to do some things independently, and other things with your supervision. Many 2- and 3-year-olds can begin to use knives to cut vegetables (softer ones at first, like mushrooms or tomatoes). They can all help to stir muffins or cookie dough. Some older preschoolers may be able to roll out cookie dough and use cookie cutters to make cookie shapes. Vary the cooking projects between ones they need your help with, and ones they can do independently.

Try:

- Muffins (mom's help -- try setting all the measured ingredients out on the table with a bowl and spoon and allowing them to "do it alone")
- Slicing soft fruit or veggies (mom's help at first)
- Graham cracker-and-nut-butter sandwiches (independent -- offer nuts, raisins, marshmallows, etc. for decorating)
- Fruit pizza (mom makes the crust -- kids can spread on cream cheese, layer on fruit)
- Pizza (mom makes the crust -- kids add tomato sauce, cheese, toppings)
- Smoothies (kids add items to the blender; help mom push the right buttons)
- Cookie decorating (mom makes the cookies -- kids add the frosting, sprinkles, etc.)
- Sandwiches (mom sets out the ingredients -- cheese, meat, veggies, nut butter, etc. -- kids make the sandwiches)
- Pretzels and marshmallows to make "snowmen" (use the pretzels to hold the marshmallows together -- kids can do this independently)

Don't be afraid to go out on a limb and teach your child to make one of your family's favorite dishes, if she's interested.

Play Dough/Clay

Play dough will become much more sophisticated at this time. Smaller children mostly just squish it and maybe throw it, but older children will want to make "stuff" out of it. Offer some play dough, or some type of safe modeling clay (some of it is toxic, so read the label carefully). You can even find recipes online to make your own -- the most successful ones include flour, water, oil, salt, and cream of tartar. Give them lots of different tools:

- Butter knives
- Rolling pin
- Toothpicks or coffee stirers
- Bowls
- Cookie sheets
- Cookie cutters

Consider keeping some of their creations, by allowing them to air dry, or to dry in the oven on 250 for several hours (check to make sure it doesn't burn). Homemade salt dough may be a good alternative to playdough for keep creations. Older children may want to make things like beads (use the toothpicks to create holes) and use the finished/dried beads to make jewelry!

Arts and Crafts Time

Offer your child a chance to do open-ended arts and crafts. Provide a space that can get messy, and offer a few or several of these materials:

- Paper (regular, parchment, construction, etc.)
- Crayons
- Markers
- Paints
- Glue or glue sticks
- Glitter or "sparkles"

- Beads (large ones are better at this age)
- Feathers
- Pipe cleaners
- Scissors
- Tape
- "Found" items (coffee filters, old boxes, paper bags, paper plates, clean empty bottles, etc.)

Allow your child to "create" as they desire! You can offer suggestions for projects, or allow them to come up with their own ideas. Many children are very creative! The younger ones will often just  scribble on paper for a few minutes (around age 2) but older kids can build or create very elaborate projects if they're allowed the time and space.

Be sure to do "art" in a room that can get messy. Try doing it outside if the weather cooperates, or cover your kitchen table in newspapers. Toddlers are very messy with markers, paints, and glue. If you aren't up for a huge mess, you can limit it to paper and crayons at times. Try to allow the messier/more creative art time now and then, though!

Puppet-Making and Show

Many children enjoy puppets and puppet shows. If you have "real" puppets (Melissa & Doug makes very nice ones), those are a great option. Or, your child can use small brown paper bags to make their own puppets. Choose a low table with a cloth over it, or a box with a hole cut in the side as a "stage" for the show, and allow your child to act out a favorite story or create their own. Or, get in on the action and do it with them!

Legos or Duplos

A lot of children enjoy playing with blocks. The younger kids (from about 18 months to age 3) do better with Duplos, which are larger and easier to put together. Older children, starting around age 3 - 4, can sometimes use the smaller Legos. Children can build whatever they like! Buildings, designs, spaceships, etc. Some kids like the "kits" that come with instructions on how to build specific things, while others prefer an open-ended box of assorted pieces. Choose what your child prefers or do some of both.

Reading Books

There's always good old-fashioned books! Offer your child a variety of books -- board books they can "read" alone, fairy tales, early readers, etc. Consider a bookshelf for your favorites and trips to the library for new stories every week or two. Give your child time to explore books by themselves (a cozy corner with big pillows and blankets is inviting) and spend time reading to them each day, too. Many children learn to read eventually because they are read to.

Dolls

Dolls aren't just for girls. Both boys and girls will probably grow up to be parents, and can "practice" on baby dolls. Offer a variety of different dolls, especially if your child shows an interest, plus blankets, diapers, clothes, a baby bed, and other accessories. This is also good if a new sibling shows up, as children can safely take out any confused or unhappy feelings on a doll, rather than the real baby.

Make-Believe

Encourage children to "play pretend." Many children learn to understand the world around them by acting out ideas that they have seen. Perhaps they will mimic a favorite TV show, or something that happened at a play date recently. Some children will make up complete fantasy scenarios to play! Some have imaginary friends, or like to take on different personas (like being a dog, or a monster). Encourage this sort of play and if they ask, play a role in the game!

Cars and Trucks

Many young children are into cars and trucks -- either large ones they can ride, or small ones they can "drive." Choose a car rug, or use a big piece of cardboard to make your own "track" for them -- encourage the child to draw a road and whatever else they like (make small buildings, trees, etc.) and then play on it. Or, put a piece of cardboard tipped up and use it as a ramp. Let the child get creative with it!

Gardening/Treasure Hunts

Getting outside to dig in the dirt or sand is often a child's pleasure. If you don't have or want a sandbox, consider allocating a little patch of land that is just for digging in the dirt (and steer your child away from any "real" gardens you are growing!). Some children like to bury and then "find treasure" in the dirt. Some like to notice rocks and worms. Some enjoy using the dirt to make "mud pies" or other concoctions. Some like to actually plant seeds and have a little garden. Many like to do all of these things! Provide small shovels, buckets, sifters, etc. for your child to use. Having some safe "treasures" to buy (small cars, hard balls, etc.) is good too if your child enjoys this.

You can also create a treasure/scavenger hunt for your child, if they're interested. We have done a treasure hunt that included things like "find 10 dandelions" and "get 7 sticks." These were items that we found around our yard or neighborhood. Or, you can hide a particular item and create a picture-based "map" for them to use to search for the item.

Puzzles

Many children enjoy putting together puzzles. There are the very simple wooden ones where each piece fits into its own spot. Then there are puzzles that have 10 - 25 pieces that older kids may want to put together. Choose the ones that your child most enjoys, and sit together to do them if needed.

Educational Videos

A lot of people write off TV as "useless" or even "bad," but kids can learn quite a lot from it, if the shows are carefully chosen and children don't spend all day watching! We've been surprised at times what our children have learned! Try some of the following shows:

- Magic School Bus
- How It's Made
- Reading Rainbow
- Wild Kratts
- Fireman Sam (my 2-year-old's favorite)
- Mister Rogers
- Super Why
- Team Umizoomi
- Bob the Builder

Unschooling Materials

The best materials at this age are open-ended and allow a lot of exploration. They also need to be safe, so that constant supervision isn't required to use them. The younger kids in this age bracket may still put items in their mouths often, so be careful about what you choose.

Good ideas include:

- Wooden blocks (both square-only and varying shapes and sizes)
- Duplos and/or Legos
- Art supplies
- Pattern blocks or "shape" blocks
- Puppets
- Dolls and accessories
- Play kitchen and accessories
- Scarves (large ones, which can become anything when pretending)
- Books
- Play dough
- Balls (various sizes and purpose -- kicking balls, soft foam throwing balls, etc.)
- Bikes or trikes
- Slides
- Cars or trucks
- Wooden trains

- Large board or cardboard for making a "track" for cars
- Marble mazes (3+)
- Digging/gardening tools
- Working "tools" (quality, kid-safe hammers, nails, screwdrivers, etc. and a piece of scrap wood)
- Small wooden table and chairs
- Puzzles

What Our Family Does At This Age

At this age, our family spends a lot of time allowing free play. Kids are encouraged to go outside when possible, to dig in the dirt or to play ball, or ride bikes. When they're inside, we offer a lot of puzzles, blocks, simple games, art supplies, and more. Most of the time, they are engaged in one or two favorite activities. For our current 3-year-old, that's usually Duplos, or sometimes art. He also really loves tools and pretending to "fix" or "build" things.

We read together sometimes, depending on interest. We also offer educational TV shows especially when we all need to calm down!

Although we do not push academics at this age, we do start to offer certain learning games, songs, and books closer to age 4. We pick up workbooks at places like dollar stores, we have puzzles, counting manipulatives, cute Youtube videos, etc. The Youtube channel ABC123 has a lot of videos that our kids like on a variety of topics.

We also often go to local children's museums, metro parks, and other local educational places and encourage exploration there. We spend a lot of time engaged in play of various types!

Section 3:
Unschooling Age 4 - 6

This is the age where most people start to really think about "school." Most kids would be starting kindergarten in this age range, and some will even go on to first grade. A lot of families feel like they need to start "learning more" or pushing academics.

However, studies show that before age 7, academics are really not necessary or beneficial. Many children will begin to learn to read, write, and do basic math at this time anyway, and children who have a specific interest should be encouraged! Sit-down lessons to try to "teach" these concepts with workbooks, flashcards, etc. are still not necessary (but can be helpful if a child latches on to these ideas on their own).

It's hard, sometimes, because there can be so much pressure to start doing "real school" at this age, from society, from friends, from parents. We can psych ourselves out, even, wondering if our children are really learning anything!

The first thing to do is relax. Then keep reading to find out what's happening at this age!

What Unschooling Looks Like Now

As I mentioned in the intro, this is the age when formal academics would usually start, and you may feel pressure to do so too. But rest assured, this is not necessary for children to continue learning, and even pick up basic reading, writing, and math skills without any formal instruction.

An interesting study (http://ecrp.uiuc.edu/v4n1/marcon.html) shows that while children in early academically-driven programs "succeed" better in the first few years of school (success being defined by higher grades in math and reading), by  the time they are in late elementary school, they actually do less well. Once the "basics" have been mastered and more creative, abstract thought is required, these students begin to struggle.

In our opinion, the basics will be learned no matter what. Children are steeped in the need for basic math, reading, and writing skills daily. A child can't pick up a book to learn about an interesting topic, follow a recipe, etc. if they can't read. The same goes with math -- it's needed for grocery shopping, budgeting, counting items, doubling or halving recipes, and so on. These skills will come.

What won't necessarily come -- what can actually be trained out -- is the creative, independent problem solving. When students are taught from a young age to simply do things a specific way every time, they learn what they are taught. This study (http://www.sciencedirect.com/science/article/pii/S0010027710002258) shows that children who were given a new toy and allowed to discover it played with it in more ways and discovered more functions than children who were specifically instructed in how to use the toy.

Another study (http://www.sciencedirect.com/science/article/pii/S0010027710002921) showed that when children were shown a particular sequence of actions to produce a specific result, they would follow this sequence exactly each time if instructed in an "educational" manner, but if they were shown at random, they would develop a shorter sequence of actions to produce the same result -- innovating instead of imitating.

These are good information to share with others who may question if unschooling is able to actually "educate" a child -- of course it can!

The information clearly shows that continuing to allow free exploration and child-led learning is the better way to produce quality results in terms of learning.

However, one thing you will need to do more of is help to

satisfy their curiosity. Children this age begin to ask a lot of questions. They will need you to help them get answers to those questions. This may mean reading books to them, or bringing books that they can read themselves, or looking up educational videos, or visiting museums. You may not even know the answers to all their questions, and will discover new information together! Frequent conversations about what is on their minds are also great -- many children learn a lot from these.

Participating in more activities with others, whether formally or informally, is a good idea now too. There are homeschooling groups, gym classes, art classes, sports teams, etc. -- choose a couple that interest your child.

You will spend more time on projects now, mostly likely. Some children have very specific things in mind that they want to accomplish, and may ask for specific materials and support in order to accomplish them. Help your child get what they need, if the request is feasible.

Independent play is balanced by parental guidance and help -- but it's still child-led.

If there's a particular subject that you want your child to study, like music or art or a foreign language, unless your child shows a special interest, hold off until at least age 7. By this time, children are more able and willing to try new things, study specifically, and follow directions. But, consider how important this is to you. If your child does not share the interest, forcing the study may frustrate both of you. That's up to you though!

Developmental Goals

• •

At this age, developmental goals diverge a little bit from "mainstream" goals -- for some children. For example, most children learn to read between ages 3 and 9, so it may or may not happen in this age range. The mainstream, however, wants children to all know how to read by the end of kindergarten or certainly first grade. If your child does achieve this goal, then great. If not, no need to be concerned.

- Develop cooperative play, rather than just parallel play
- The ability to imagine scenarios and act them out or tell them as a story
- Creative, multi-step problem solving
- Speaking clearly and in full sentences, mostly correct grammar
- Knows first and last name, parents' names
- Classifies objects by groups (shape, color, size, etc.)
- Recognizing letters and letter sounds
- Counting to 100 (or so)
- Basic addition (single digit or up to sums of 20)
- Early reading
- Improved fine-motor control (holding a pencil or crayon, using scissors, zippers and buckles, etc.)
- Improved gross-motor control (climbing, running, jumping, pumping on the swing, riding a bike)
- Independent play

- Self-control

Your child may do some or most of these. It is likely that your child will reach some of these by age 3 and some not until 7 or later -- this is normal! These are just general guidelines that many children reach around this age. The older they get, the wider the range of development. Everyone has different talents and some areas will come easily and some will not.

Don't get caught up in the "comparison game" and remember that each child is an individual. Plus, early "academic success" is not predictive of lifelong success!

Unschooling Activities

At this age, there are as many activities as there are children! So much is driven by their interests. I'll suggest several general activities and include some of our family's favorites, but don't be afraid to go above and beyond this and listen to your child. The older they get, the more individual it all is.

Arts and Crafts

As before, provide a variety of arts and crafts supplies for your child. By this age, they should be less messy and also less likely to put items in their mouths, so they can have a wider variety of supplies. Offer:

- Paper (white, construction, parchment, etc.)
- Tissue paper
- Crayons
- Markers
- Colored Pencils
- Pencils/pens

- Glue
- Tape
- Scissors
- Hole punch
- Cardboard boxes/cartons
- Empty, clean plastic jars and bottles
- Beads
- String or yarn
- Pieces of small craft wood
- T-shirts
- Felt
- Paper plates
- Foam balls
- Wooden or foam "wreath" forms

At this age, children may have an interest in painting shirts, tie-dyeing, creating musical instruments from plates, bottles, beads, etc. and more complicated crafts. They can make ornaments out of salt dough. Glue can make window clings. Simple glue in water (roughly equal parts) and newspaper can make items of out papier-mache.

1. Try making window clings that are seasonal.

2. Act out a favorite story (make the characters and "sets").

3. Create a solar system from papier-mache.

4. Use a balloon as the center of your papier-mache and create your own pinata in your child's favorite shape/

object. (Cover the balloon with strips of wet newspaper, decorate with paint and/or tissue paper, and use a small pin to pop the balloon later.)

5. Use salt dough to make a map of a real place, or a fantasy land from your child's imagination.

6. Make hand prints or bite prints in salt dough to study parts of the human body.

7. Create play "food" from felt, wood, or salt dough and let your child sew or paint it.

8. Create a seasonal or other themed wreath.

9. Make jewelry with beads and string, and practice sorting and patterns.

10. Use cardstock and tissue paper to make a "stained glass window" in a variety of patterns.

11. Cut snowflakes from white paper and use as decorations.

12. Take a square of paper and draw an interesting shape that goes diagonally across it (roughly). Cut along the shape, then glue the cut part to the back of it. This will create a template to allow your child to create designs on paper that fit perfectly together.

There are endless projects here!

Cooking Projects

Kids this age are starting to be able to do a lot more in the kitchen. The actual projects suggested in the 2 - 4 age group are all still valid, but they'll be able to do more of the work themselves now. Skills most kids in this age have or will develop include:

- Using knives to slice fruits and veggies (and possibly cheese)
- Using the stove to cook simple meals -- ground meat, scrambled eggs, pancakes, etc. (with adult supervision!)
- Following recipes for muffins or other simple recipes mostly independently
- Make smoothies or ice cream
- Many projects the child can do alone, with your guidance and support.

1. Try making "ice cream" in a bag! Mix the ingredients in a blender (milk, cream, egg yolks, sugar, vanilla) and then pour into a Ziploc-style bag. Put the bag in a bowl of ice and scrunch and mix it every now and then until it's frozen.

2. Kids can also make homemade butter -- pour heavy cream into a jar and put the lid on. Sometimes, adding a clean marble helps make this easier. Shake the cream until it thickens into butter! Kids can then learn to "wash" the butter (by mixing with cold water and mashing it around until the water runs clear) and salt the butter before eating it. This is a good lesson in what agitation does to cream.

3. You can follow up by beating eggs or egg whites to see what happens to those, and if you choose egg whites, make macaroon cookies.

Excavation

The "digging in the dirt" that littler ones do can lead to a lesson in people who dig in dirt for a living! There are several kits in school supply stores that allow kids to practice excavation, for fool's gold, cheap gemstones, etc. (These can vary from $2 to $20 depending on the size.)

Or, you can visit a local creek bed and try some real excavation -- you may find fossils or arrowheads. You can even set up an excavation by burying specific items in dirt and sand and then allowing your child to dig them out, brush them off, and wash them. Videos or books on archaeologists and what they find are a great complement to this lesson.

For children who are strongly interested in this, cards about dinosaurs or specific artifacts, books on archaeology, a visit to a natural history museum, a short meeting with a real archaeologist, etc. would be great follow-ups.

Geo Tracking

Some children love a "treasure hunt." Try finding a geo tracking app in your area and use GPS to help locate a "treasure" and then bury one of your own. Kids can learn about how GPS works and how to follow directions and co-ordinates, as well as how to dig and unearth the "treasures" that geo tracking allows. If your child is interested, you can even create your own new hidden treasures in new areas for others to find!

Solar System

Many children have an interest in planets and the solar system. There are several hands-on ways to explore this.

Create a model of the solar system out of papier-mache or using foam balls. If you're really brave, try making a scale model (it's really hard. There are calculators online, but if the smallest planet is only 1 cm, the largest planet is still a couple feet in diameter). Kids can color, paint, or otherwise decorate the planets. Some choose to make the sun as a lantern so that it can light up, and show how the sun lights the moon and creates a shadow on the Earth.

Purchase or make stars -- glow-in-the-dark ones are neat -- and put them up on the walls and ceiling of a room. Make constellations out of them and talk about what these are. Visit a planetarium to see the constellations, or get a telescope and go outside to see the real ones. Some kids prefer to draw, cut, and color their own stars (you could purchase glow-in-the-dark paint if you like!).

Find or buy moon rocks and other rock/material samples to represent the planets. Talk about what they are made of -- rocks, metals, and gases.

There are a number of excellent interactive books, and sticker books, about the planets which can help kids learn their names and basic characteristics of them. The Youtube channel ABC123 also has a few songs about the planets.

Human Body

Many kids have a fascination with their bodies. Kids as young as 18 months can start to name body parts, but older kids will be interested in how their bodies actually work -- what's on the inside?

Creating models of the body can be fun -- kids can use salt dough to create bones and make a skeleton. They can trace their own bodies on paper and draw color them in (with clothes, hair, etc. or they can just draw bones, or muscles, etc.). Magic School Bus makes a couple of different shows about the human body, one on the digestive system and one on the immune system.

There are lot of excellent videos on Youtube about the body as well -- cute little songs about bones, muscles, etc.

Conversations about how muscles work are fun. Practice dancing, jumping, or throwing a ball and explain how muscles make that possible. Have them make a "strong arm" and squeeze their muscles -- or show them yours or Dad's after the gym!

Kids can feel their bones, too -- try at the wrist or elbow, where the bones are easier to feel. Look at how knees and elbows bend and talk about bones and muscles working together.

Some kids are freaked out by blood, but you can make "blood" with tomato juice and try moving it through straws or tubes and talk about how it moves through your body like that. Use a toy stethoscope or lay your head on another person's chest to hear their heart and talk about how the

heart pumps the blood through the body. (Take the tomato juice and straws outside and practice sucking it up and
blowing it out -- the heart does both motions! -- but this is
messy.)

Kids can use different foods to represent internal organs
and feel what they are like. Try buying a calf's liver to talk
about your liver and what it is for. Use kidney beans to talk
about kidneys. Strawberries can represent hearts. Walnuts
look like small brains. Use raw meat to talk about muscles
-- since that's what it is!

Culture probiotics and talk about gut flora. Build models of
the body and show the placement of internal organs.

If you are having a new baby and kids are curious about
this, consider watching birth videos. There are some excellent ones on Youtube. Many are quite graphic, so decide
what you want your children to see and pre-screen them if
you are concerned. We chose to be very upfront with our
children about this and allowed them to watch the graphic
videos (with us at their side) from a young age.

There are so many ways to study this, depending on what
your child is interested in. Bones, muscles, and skin are the
basics, but you can study what the eyes do, what the intes-
tines do, how babies grow inside, and more.

Dancing

Many children love to dance. The average child can simply dance to whatever music is playing. Try playing clas-
sical selections, rock selections -- basically lots of different

styles and tempos for kids to move to. Some may choose to stomp/march in time to the music. Others may just like moving around.

Kids with a strong interest in dance may be interested in videos about basic dance moves, or dance classes.

Of course, it may not be dance your child is into, but a different sport or physical activity. At this age, a class or team may be a good idea, although it's probably a good idea to start with a 4 to 6-week introductory course to make sure they are interested before committing to a whole season or year.

Water Exploration

While little kids just like to play with water, older kids can actually experiment with it.

1. Try measuring water and seeing how much it weighs.

2. Freeze the measured water and see if there is more or less of it (by volume) than before -- frozen water should expand.

3. Melt an ice cube in the refrigerator, on the counter, and in a pot on the stove and see how long each takes and talk about why.

4. Put an ice cube into a tray of water and see if it sinks or floats!

5. Measure water and pour it into a different container with a totally different shape. Talk about how the amount of water is the same even though it looks dif-

ferent.

6. Fill a bucket or sink with water and get a bunch of different objects. Find out if they float or sink and talk about why. Try setting a small bowl or cup on the water (which should float), then fill it with water and watch it sink.

7. Mix different things into the water and see if it changes color, or if the texture feels different (salt water should feel different).

8. Try dissolving salt or sugar in water and see how much you can add before it no longer works, and talk about "concentration."

9. Dissolve salt in water that is cold, room temperature, and warm and see which is easiest and why.

10. Set up three containers of water -- cold, room temperature and warm (not hot enough to burn, but pretty warm). Have your child place their hands in the cold and "hot" ones for a minute, then put both into the room temperature water and feel how different it is on the two hands! This is a good lesson in how nerves work, too.

What Freezes?

Find out what actually freezes! (Make sure that your littles know that not everything here is edible!)

Try freezing:

- Regular water

- Salt water
- Isopropyl alcohol or vodka
- Hydrogen peroxide
- Honey
- Any other liquid you have that isn't toxic(pure juices are interesting -- many will freeze, but remain a bit tacky)

1. Find out what does freeze and what doesn't. Time them to see how long they take! (Both regular and salt water should freeze, the alcohol shouldn't. Salt water takes longer than regular water.)

2. Try seeing how long each takes to melt.

3. Pour rock salt onto a pan of shallow ice (freeze a 9x13 baking pan with ½" of water or less) and see what this does to the ice.

4. See if you can find something that helps melt the ice faster. What happens when you pour hot water onto it?

5. Try mixing water with some of the other liquids and freezing those. Do they freeze now? Try different combinations, like 1:1 water to alcohol, 1:2, etc. and see when it stops freezing.

6. Mix together juice and water (or lemon juice, water, and sugar) and put it in a Ziploc bag and stick it in the freezer. Try two bags. The first bag, allow to freeze completely. The second bag, remove every 15 minutes and shake/mix with your hands (on the outside of the bag). See what happens to the two bags after a couple hours. If you have an ice cream maker, try running a

third recipe through the ice cream maker. Talk about the action of churning, adding air during the freezing process and what this does -- eat your results!

What is Magnetic?

1. Get a small magnet -- a magnet bar or circle, something they can grip easily (not like a flat refrigerator magnet that businesses give away). Carry it around the house and see what it sticks to! It will stick to most metal, but not wood, although it won't stick to stainless steel. Talk about what metal is and isn't magnetic.

2. Try sticking two magnets together. Try them different ways, north-south, and north-north, south-south. See how the north-north and south-south actually repel each other instead of sticking together! Talk about the magnetic poles.

3. If you're brave, get some stronger magnets and see what they can do. Be careful, fingers can get pinched! Try some mag-lev trains -- they're powered just by the magnets and you can build them yourself. (How to build your own model: http://www.kidscanpress.com/machinesofthefuture/pdf_activities/UltTra_OnlineProject.pdf)

Math Jumping

A lot of kids will like this game, because it teaches math but it is very physical!

Use a long sheet of paper (or tape several together) to create a giant number line -- put a good 12" between each number. Have your child pick a number to stand on to start. Then, choose a second number (single digit). You can make one up, have your child throw a rock onto a number chart, spin some sort of dial, etc. Have your child move up that many numbers. So, for example, if they start at 1, and the next number is 3, they will move up 3 spaces and land on 4. Then you can say, "1 + 3 = 4!" This same concept can be used for simple subtraction problems.

You can also make a smaller number line and use Lego bricks, beans, etc. to do this same sort of thing on a table instead of jumping around.

Yeast

Explore what yeast does. If you bake bread, your kids may know what it is, but not what it really does!

1. First, pour some dry yeast into three small bowls. In one, leave it dry. In another, add just water. In the third, add water and sugar. See what happens to each after 10 minutes! (The first two should basically stay the same, while the third will get puffy and foamy.) Talk about how sugar is food for the yeast, and the yeast produce gases as they consume their food.

2. Try this experiment again inside of bottle and put balloons on top -- the sugar/yeast/water combination will begin to inflate the balloon, but the others won't.

3. Follow up by making bread. Try very small recipes with no yeast, some yeast, and a lot of yeast. See what

happens to the different bread (try mini-loaves). Taste them after they are baked to see how they look and taste different.

4. Mention how yeast lives in our bodies, too. Try some yeast-based fermentations, like kombucha.

5. Look at pictures of different strains of yeast under a microscope.

Chemistry

Try different chemistry experiments!

1. There's the classic vinegar + baking soda. Try mixing different amounts together to see what happens -- if the reaction lasts longer or shorter, if there's any of either chemical left over at the end and why.

2. You can also mix 1 c. of hydrogen peroxide with a few drops of dish soap, then add a combination of 1 tsp. yeast + 2 tbsp. hot water. This will foam up and create a huge, cool reaction -- it's messy! Both this and the vinegar/baking soda are "exothermic."

3. Try putting a raw egg into a bowl of vinegar and letting it sit. The outer shell will dissolve, leaving a "naked" egg!

4. Mix oil and water in a container with a lid (a clear container). See how they remain separate. Shake them and watch them separate again. Then, add a few drops of dish soap and shake again -- this time they should remain mixed. Soap breaks the surface tension that

normally keeps them separate.

There are a number of other experiments online similar to these, using ingredients you have commonly around the house. Try some of these: http://www.sciencekids.co.nz/experiments.html

Video Games

Some video games can be educational! Many kids play Minecraft. Others like to go on websites like www.abcmouse.com. There are plenty of interesting and educational games and websites that are interactive, depending on your child's interests. I wouldn't recommend relying heavily on these, as they're often academically-driven, but they are an interesting activity to try sometimes.

Educational TV

There is even more educational TV at this age!

- Mister Rogers
- How It's Made
- Mythbusters
- Cooking Shows
- History Channel
- Animal Planet

Look for specific shows that your child is interested in. Many shows on the Discovery channel or History channel are very interesting.

Unschooling Materials

Just like activities at this age can vary widely, so can materials. What you need will depend on your child's interests!

This is just a suggested list. Some of these things will require adult supervision, especially with the younger kids (4-year-olds need more help than 6-year-olds!).

- Art supplies
- Baking soda
- Salt
- Flour
- Hydrogen peroxide
- Yeast
- Water
- Ice trays
- Baking sheets/pans
- Large sheets of paper
- Large pieces of cardboard
- Books
- Board games (ages 3+)
- Isopropyl alcohol
- Buckets or tubs
- Magnets
- Sand
- Rocks or cheap gem stones
- Dish soap
- Towels
- Shovels

There are several more things, depending on what you want to do!

What Our Family Does At This Age

· ·

At this age, our family begins to dive into the world of "stuff." The kids participate in a local homeschool group, where they do larger-scale crafts and messy science experiments (some of the ones I listed were ones we did in our group).

We begin to read with them -- we have early readers and we sit and read to them, and ask them the words that they know. Some have been interested in sight-word flash cards, and some haven't, so we've done those with the ones that were interested.

We pull out beans and Lego blocks to use as math manipulatives. We encourage mental math skills -- the kids often start adding up various simple addition problems while we're driving. If they ask us questions like "How many blocks to I have here?" we'll encourage them to count and add.

We visit museums and we explore new areas. Rather than staying in the kids' "play" areas, we look at different exhibits and talk about what we find there. We go to the natural history museum. We travel to other kids' museums around our state sometimes. We visit historical villages.

We "excavate" with geo tracking and with small kits. We identify gemstones and other types of rocks -- what they're called and where they came from. We have books about gemstones and different types of rock. We watch videos on volcanoes and talk about volcanic rock.

We learn about parts of the body -- how our immune system works (with videos and explanations).

We decorate the house with lots of different art projects that they do. They have created robots (and robot costumes for themselves), castles, and more.

We introduce computers and allow some time playing video games. Our 5 and 7 year olds got into Minecraft last year.

We spend a lot of time building with Legos and pattern blocks. We design different structures with the Legos, including finding patterns and projects online to follow.

We cook and bake a lot and teach them to start cooking independently.

Basically, we do whatever seems awesome!

Section 4:
Unschooling Age 6+

At this age, when children are definitely "in school," the pressure to "do school at home" can become strong. If you haven't read all of the information in the introduction to the ages 4 - 6 section, go back and read it -- studies support that children are better off waiting until age 7 or later before starting "formal" study. And some students still do better without formal study even after that!

The key is remaining confident now. You know your child best and you know how s/he learns. That may mean more formal study in some areas. It may not. Letting your child's needs and interests lead is still key, and will lead to a rich education -- probably for both of you!

What Unschooling Looks Like Now

At this age, what unschooling looks like can vary quite widely.

Some children choose some subjects that strongly interest them and focus heavily on those -- spending hours reading about them, creating projects, watching videos, and so on. Others are still doing a little of this, and a little of that. Most children have some sort of passion at this point.

It should be obvious at this time what talents your child has, and what learning style your child has. The best thing that you can do, as the parent, is to help your child make goals that surround his/her passions, and suggest projects or ideas that fit his/her talents and learning style.

For example, if your child is passionate about space and rockets, and is artistically inclined, suggest using materials to build a rocket and model of the solar system to scale. Create a story book about life among the stars. Watch From the Earth to the Moon for a factual show, and watch fantasy like Doctor Who or Star Wars for the imaginary aspects. There are lots of ways to study this!

Talk to your child regularly about their interests and desires and help them create and follow through with a plan. While education is child-led, a parent's involvement is key to success. Kids can't come up with all of their own ideas, gather their materials, or execute them. Adults help them satisfy their curiosity and bring them what they need.

Sometimes your kids might have the start of an idea, but need your help, via discussion, to flesh out that idea into a project they can complete.

Make sure to work with your child, and if you have more than one, keep it individual. Don't expect a younger child to follow in an older child's footsteps -- they will have different talents and learning styles and passions, as they should. Don't compare.

Don't compare to school children, either. It's likely that in some ways your child will be ahead, and in some behind. This is normal and one of the features of homeschooling is that your child can work at his/her own pace without feeling "dumb" in the areas where they are behind the average.

Feel free to encourage reading and math skills specifically as a part of other learning projects. For example, if your child wants to build a rocket, help them figure out the correct measurements, create the pieces, and have them fit together. If you build a rocket that can fly (there are kits), then use math to figure out how high it flew and how far. Notice the wind and see if you launch in a different direction or on a day with more/less wind if the rocket flies higher or further and by how much. There's lots of math there! There will be reading, too, to figure out the instructions.

Encouraging children to notice how these skills will help them do more work, and be more independent is part of the educational process. Many will pick up on math and reading so that they can do more with their favorite projects! Share it with them, help them learn it, but don't push it if they're not ready.

Unschooling continues along a pretty steady path -- guided by your child's interests and ever-expanding abilities!

Developmental Goals

After age 6, most things will start to "click." It may be right away, it may be in a few years. Most children have a firm grasp of all the basics by 9 - 10 years of age. Many children, around 7, also begin to think in a more abstract manner and engage in higher-level discussions. Prior to this, most children are still very literal and somewhat limited in their view of the world. This is an exciting time!

You should notice:

- Develops lasting friendships with other children based on mutual interests
- Understands basic math concepts -- simple addition, subtraction, counting money, telling time
- Begins to understand abstract reasoning (around age 7 - 8)
- Begins to consider philosophical questions
- Learns to read more readily and reading skills increase over time
- Becomes more independent
- Understands the world around them
- Less selfish; more empathy for others

A lot of development is focused on relationships and the ability to think at higher levels. Development is not as striking as it was at the younger ages; it is more subtle now, but just as exciting in its own way!

Unschooling Activities

All of the activities in the 4 - 6 age range are still valid here; simply extend them a bit further for this age range. For example, take specific measurements of how much of each chemical is added to the water when seeing what will freeze, and change the ratio in smaller increments.

Rocket Ships

Build a rocket ship! There are kits to purchase online or at many hobby stores. Alternatively, you can find plans online to build your own air-powered rockets and a rocket launcher (the good part about these is that they don't require engines and can be launched several times in succession).

- Create a rocket design together, and build the rocket. Launch it and chart how high and how far it goes.
- Note the direction and speed of the wind (if possible) and theorize how this might affect the launch.
- Try creating rockets of different sizes -- widths or lengths -- and see how this affects the launch.
- Use different materials to create rockets, or different size or shape nose cones. Figure out how these affect the launch. Try to create the "best" rocket!
- Follow up by studying real rockets -- how they are powered, how they fly in space, how they return safely to earth.
- Visit a museum to see some parts of real rockets, look at books on them, and watch movies about them too.

Bridge Building

This is best for kids who are at least 7 - 8 years old.

- Watch the Magic School Bus episode about bridge building.
- Use toothpicks and graph paper to design and build a bridge.
- Try some different materials and different styles. Calculate size and scale.
- See how much weight the bridge will hold with different designs.
- Gather some friends and have a bridge-building contest!

Dissection

Dissection is a great way to learn about animals or plants around us. Almost anything simple can be dissected.

1. Try dissecting plants first -- flowers that grow in your yard are an obvious one. Try dandelions, or other "weeds." Identify the stamen, stem, leaves, and other parts of the flower, and figure out what they do.

2. Get an owl pellet from a science supply store. Have your child dissect it, saving all of the bones.

3. Try to recreate the animal's skeleton.

4. Talk about why owls create pellets.

5. Discuss the idea of dissection. Encourage your child to dissect an earthworm, too, or something similar. Older children could try dissecting a frog, a small fish, etc. -- try catching them in a local creek, or buy from a supply store.

3-D Puzzles

Choose a 3-D puzzle of your child's choice -- a historical building, spaceship, etc. (there are several choices). Work together to construct this puzzle. Once it is complete, research the item that you chose to build. When was it built? Where is it? What was/is its purpose? Who designed it? Did it work as intended? Give your child a chance to improve upon the design with wood pieces or Legos to create a new model.

Royalty

Many young girls are very interested in "princesses" -- which usually means Disney! But as they grow older, this can translate into a valid study of ancient and current royalty.

Choose a royal family or country to look at. What do they wear? Try making or buying a dress (or other garment) that is in line with their traditional style. This could be a great sewing project for kids who are interested.

What food did/do they eat? Are there are special dishes that are traditional, especially during celebrations? Find recipes for these dishes and prepare them.

What were the main jobs of the royal family? Did those change over time? Was the family controversial? Why?

What are their titles? Why? How did these titles "evolve" over time? How do people succeed to the throne?

Have they ever been challenged by a different royal family?

Were they ever overthrown -- and if so, why and who did it? Was it better for the country before or after the change of power? What can we learn from this?

Find books, videos, etc. on the family you have chosen. Look at different families in the same country to see how things changed under different rule. Try having a "royal party" and dress up in period clothes, talk in period language (if it's close to your primary language), and serve period food!

Simple Machines

Try building simple machine out of Legos, K'Nex, or simple kits. There are many plans online for building simple machines, even ones that are powered by lemons or magnets. After building a few, gather wires, scrap metal, screws, bolts, etc. and design your own simple machines.

Story Books

Create a simple book by folding paper in half and stapling it in the center. Write a story and illustrate it. If desired, use flat cardboard (like a cereal box) covered in fabric to create a pretty cover for the book. Glue the center of the book into the center of the cover after it is finished.

There are endless other ideas...follow your child's interests!

Unschooling Materials

As with the previous section, the materials in the 4 - 6 age group are still valid here. Add additional materials depending on your child's interests!

- Wood scraps
- Metal scraps
- Nails
- Screws
- Latches
- Paint
- Art supplies
- Cardboard
- Paper
- Costumes
- Puppets
- Movies
- iPad

This is just a small sampling of the possibilities!

What Our Family Does At This Age

At this time, we only have one child in this age group -- our 7-year-old. Right now, we read with her whenever she asks. We have a bunch of early reader type books that we read together, since she can read most of the words in those books. We specifically chose stories on subjects that she enjoys (mostly princesses!).

We offer a lot of different art materials, and she has her own art kit. The kit contains crayons, markers, scissors, , glue, etc. and it is her special thing, to be kept away from the little ones. She creates many different projects -- drawings, story books, cards, and more.

We still spend a lot of time visiting friends, going to museums, and so on. We hope to do more traveling and see more places as she gets older. Once she can read more complicated books, we'll help her find the ones she wants to read -- she has some cookbooks now that she wants to learn to cook from.

Basically we continue to do projects that interest her!

Section 5:
Unschooling with Other
Educational Philosophies

• •

Some people want to know -- can I combine unschooling with other schooling philosophies, like Montessori, Waldorf, etc.?

The answer is, probably.

Many educational philosophies, especially alternative ones, focus on the use of specific types of materials. Montessori focuses on child-sized tools that a grown up would use. Waldorf focuses on a lot of creative play. Both promote child-led learning.

Charlotte Mason focuses heavily on literature. This could be combined with unschooling, by doing a lot of reading. (Although admittedly I don't know much about CM philosophy; I just know several people who use it.)

Some philosophies would fly directly in the face of unschooling -- for example, any that recommended starting early academics, structure, using specific curriculum, workbooks, doing "seat work," etc. Anything that promotes parent-directed learning or academics over creative thinking is not going to be in line with unschooling and will not work with it.

However, remember that unschooling is very free. If children want to use flashcards, or workbooks, or any other materials, and they are allowed to choose those themselves and decide when/if to work with them, then it fits just fine with unschooling. That's child-directed!

Some people get caught up in this idea that children never use "traditional" materials, and never choose specific courses of study. But of course that's not true. If and when they want to, they can use any materials they want. They can choose to specifically study a particular topic and even choose their own curriculum. Many unschooled middle or high schoolers do get to this point. Probably most.

The only key tenet of unschooling is "child-led." Really. Whatever else you focus on or don't focus on, or whatever materials you use or don't use, doesn't qualify or disqualify you as an unschooler. This is not a rigid philosophy.

If you choose, at any point, that it is better for your family to have some parent-directed activities, then that's your right as well. Some families feel that unschooling is good in the early years, but by age 7 - 8 they would prefer something more formal for math and reading. Some kids feel the need to have structure and curriculum and others like to just "do what comes." Know your child and choose what's going to work best for you. If that's more structure, then so be it.

This is about what's best for your family. It's never a good idea to follow a particular philosophy because it "seems" like a good idea. Honestly examine and re-examine what's working for you and what isn't, and throw out what isn't and find another way. There are so many choices out there.

Made in the USA
San Bernardino, CA
17 March 2016